Always Dream Big

Dream Girl

Jurnee

Dream Board in a Book:
A Modern Day Guide to Your Glamorous Life

Yvette E. Tariq/MUSABooks, LLC.

Washington, DC/20019

bit.ly/thetariqsphere

Cover Design by: Yvette E. Tariq
Book Design by: Yvette E. Tariq
Page Design and Layout by: Yvette E. Tariq

Dream Board in a Book: A Modern Day Guide to Your Glamorous Life.
 -- 1st ed.

ISBN 978-0-9964330-2-0

Mom & Dad thank you for encouraging my creative mind, loving me, and believing in all of my dreams. I love you! To B.Brown, my main man, my stepdad, thank you for being the perfect addition. I love you just the same!

To my husband Mustafa, you are my partner in everything, your love for me is the greatest gift. #inthetrenches

To my son Evrence, eat your vegetables!

To my family, I love you all, keep dreaming.

To Patricia Odham, your spirit is amazing, you will always be a leading example and inspiration in my life.

WELCOME TO YOUR GLAMOROUS LIFE

Hey Love,

Dream Board in a Book is here to empow-HER you one page at a time. This Glam Guide will encourage you to tap into your most glamorous thoughts, put them out into the universe, and prosper...and you'll do all this by using the law of attraction! Dream Board in a Book encourages you to recognize the power you have over your experience. Its time for you to detox all things negative and make room for that which we know you deserve.

-Yvette E. Tariq

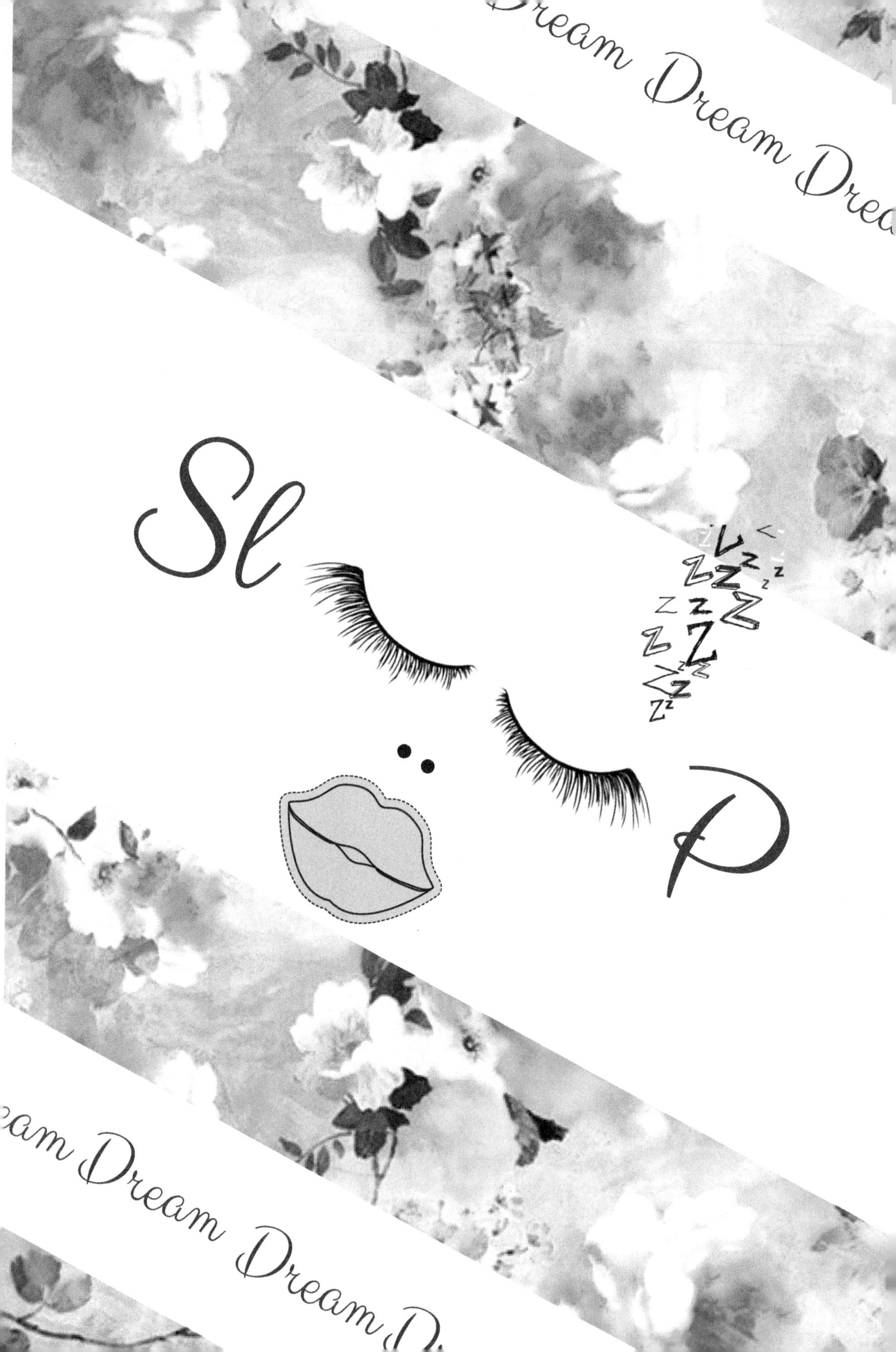
Dream Dream
Sl p
Dream Dream

"Ma'am would you like to view our classic double flap?" a slender framed young lady asked as she held a gorgeous fuchsia pink lambskin handbag against your hip. The chain sparkled perfectly next to your diamond encrusted bezel. Convinced, you decided to fancy around a little more, taking in the handbag's decadant flair. Making your way to the register you were interrupted by an absurd alarm. It startled everyone in the store, especially you, right out of your sleep!

Oftentimes, we experience an infinite power within our dreams that we wish transferred into our reality. While getting our beauty rest we can win the most difficult of battles as a ruling Queen, and in the very next instance we are jet setting into a new time zone for the shopping spree of a lifetime. Only, a lifetime seems to be everyday when you are in a dream state.

A dream can be so captivating, awaking from it will have you trying to get right back to where you left off. Stop waiting until you close your eyes to chase after your dreams and start making them your reality. We all possess one thing inside of us that guarantees success, and that my darling is ability. The ability to succeed at whatever we put our minds to. But first, lets begin the process of speaking those dreams into existence. Lets get them out of your head, and into your Dream Board in a Book!

WHO ARE YOU?

DO TELL...

How do I know if he's really the one!?
I think I want to marry him but I'm
not sure if he's going to open up to
me.

DO   TELL...

Check

your

baggage

at

the

door...

Don't allow that extra baggage to anchor you down. You were meant to soar!

-Yvette E. Tariq

Sort through your baggage and look for the uncluttered glam; the parts that truly make you who you are. Uncover the important things that have become submerged in anguish, and rid yourself of what is left.

At times we believe we are protecting ourselves with the things that we hold onto. In all actuality, that dead weight is only dictating your existence. It will never allow you to flourish in your destiny.

Release for your relief.
No longer will you hide behind fears, doubt, and uncertainty!

Anxiety

Doubt

Laziness

Quiting M.S. mindset

Dishonesty

Shame

Gossip

Financial Hardships

Unpack Here!
fill each bag & let it go

6/2/19
Isolation

5/8/20
Bitterness?

5/8/20
Big Mouth

Hey Glammy...

It's time
to start

dreaming

The Law of Attraction

Believing in the law of attraction is believing wholeheartedly that you are a magnet in your life. You know that you have authority over all things positive and negative. "How ?" you ask, BY having faith and backing it with action, that's how. Your belief is what aligns your steps to receive. NOW as for Negativity its simple, do NOT put forth any of your energy towards it.

The
Law of
Attraction

Give thanks daily as if you've
already received your universal
requests. Even on your not so
great days, treat them as
if they were your best days.
Your gratitude and patience
will be the key to your success.
Continue working through your
dream board in a book and bring
forth the best into fruition.
You deserve it!

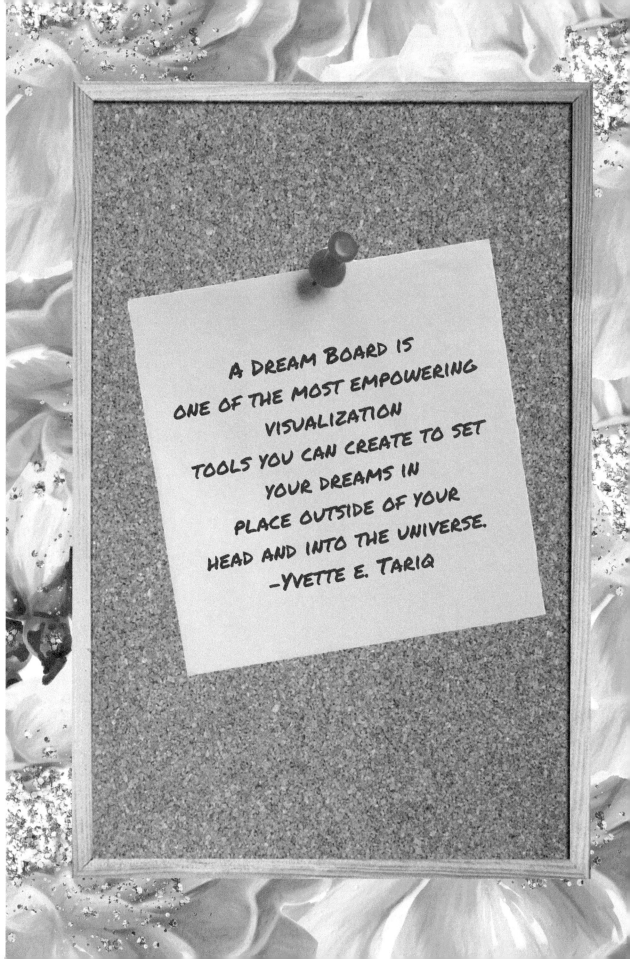

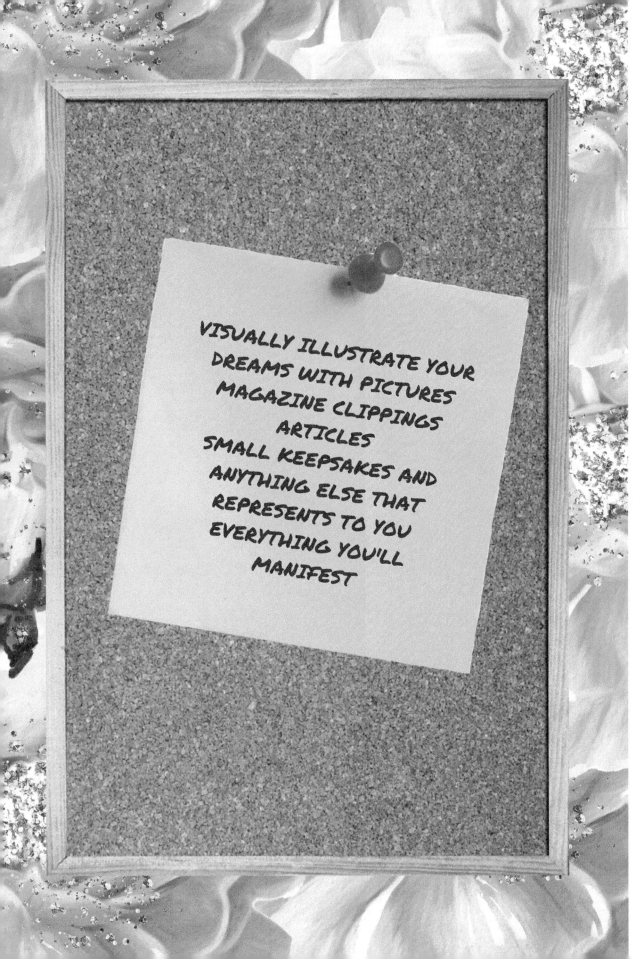

AFFIRM YOUR GREATNESS

AFFIRM YOUR GREATNESS

FAITH

+

ACTION

=

YOUR DREAMS COME TRUE

My Goals

List your goal below and the steps you must take in order to see it achieved.

Goal: Purge Nails

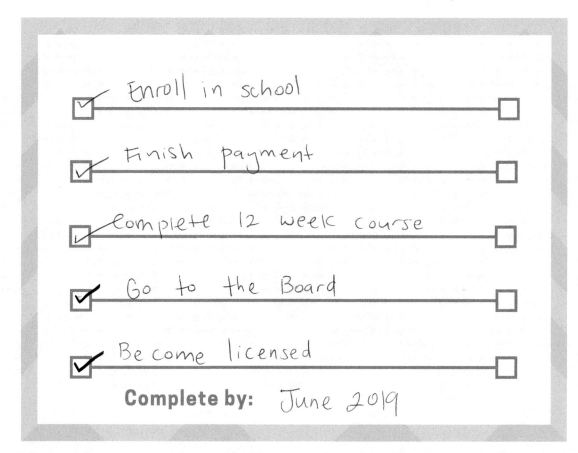

- ☑ Enroll in school ☐
- ☑ Finish payment ☐
- ☑ Complete 12 week course ☐
- ☑ Go to the Board ☐
- ☑ Become licensed ☐

Complete by: June 2019

This goal is important for me to achieve because...

Purge Nails equals financial security, Completion of a goal, Answered prayer from God, and that I'm walking in my purpose.

Dec. 2023

became licence but didn't truly pursue with more practice and faithy confidence building 2024 will be the year I begin nails

My Goals

List your goal below and the steps you must take in order to see it achieved.

Goal: Optimum Health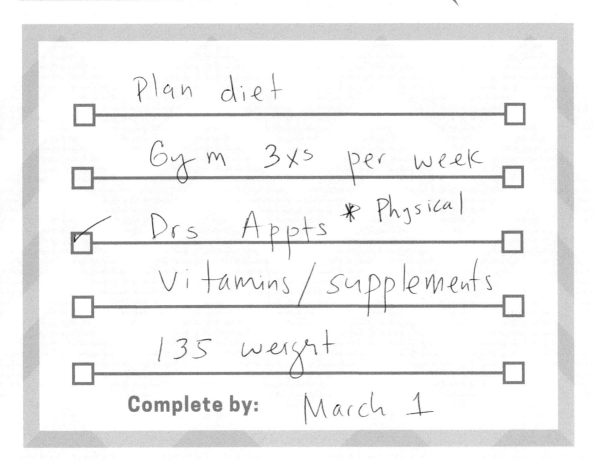

- Plan diet
- Gym 3xs per week
- ☑ Drs Appts * Physical
- Vitamins / supplements
- 135 weight

Complete by: March 1

This goal is important for me to achieve because...

[2023] went to the gym also canceling membership 2024 January I will be in the gym a few times a week until membership ends

My Goals

List your goal below and the steps you must take in order to see it achieved.

Goal: Complete 90 days in the bible app

- Open the app first thing in the morning
- Really dive into plans
- Take notes

Complete by: July 11 2019

This goal is important for me to achieve because...

I want to know Gods word in order to draw closer to him and apply the word to my life.   2023 Accomplished
177 days stopped plan in June
will try again 2024

My Goals

2023 december my finances are completely a mess will be starting a new position but I'm Starting over to clear debt 2024

List your goal below and the steps you must take in order to see it achieved.

Goal: Save 3500$

☐ Stop spending money on things I dont need ☐
☐ Save money every time I earn money ☐
☐ ☐
☐ ☐
☐ ☐

Complete by: 12/31/19

This goal is important for me to achieve because...

I want to create a financial cushion. I want to start the year of 2020 off with a minimum of 3500$ saved.

My Goals

I've been offered another opportunity to become a merchandiser this time I will remember to be grateful for all I have and appreciative that I was blessed with another chance

List your goal below and the steps you must take in order to see it achieved.

Goal: Find Merchandising Employment and start working

- [ ] Complete Resume
- [ ] Send off to multiple Jobs
- [ ] Check up on the jobs
- [ ] Start work
- [ ] Get my first Pay check

Complete by: July 31st

This goal is important for me to achieve because...

This goal was Accomplished on time. Less than 30 days into my position I started to take it for granted forgetting it was exactly what I prayed and asked for.

My Goals

List your goal below and the steps you must take in order to see it achieved.

Goal: Product launching
(Bitters, hair oil, cuticle oil)

☐ Buy liquor ☐

☐ Find herbs ☐

☐ package oil ☐

☐ Find stickers ☐

☐ set up display (post) ☐

Complete by: Oct 12 th

This goal is important for me to achieve because...

I no longer want to pursue this path but I have gained more talents that later on I maybe be able to launch a successful product line! Not right now.
2023 december

HEALTHY IS **EAT GREEN**
THE NEW SEXY

DRINK WATER

EAT
VEGETABLES

EXERCISE

THINK POSITIVE

MIND YOUR
BUSINESS

As you prepare yourself for a life you don't need a vacation from, you'll begin to notice one thing...not everyone is meant to embark on this journey with you. That's right, its time to cut those loose ends. Be very honest with yourself, and list those who do not deserve a seat at your table.

NEVER RELY ON AN
OUTSIDE SOURCE
FOR YOUR
INTERNAL HAPPINESS

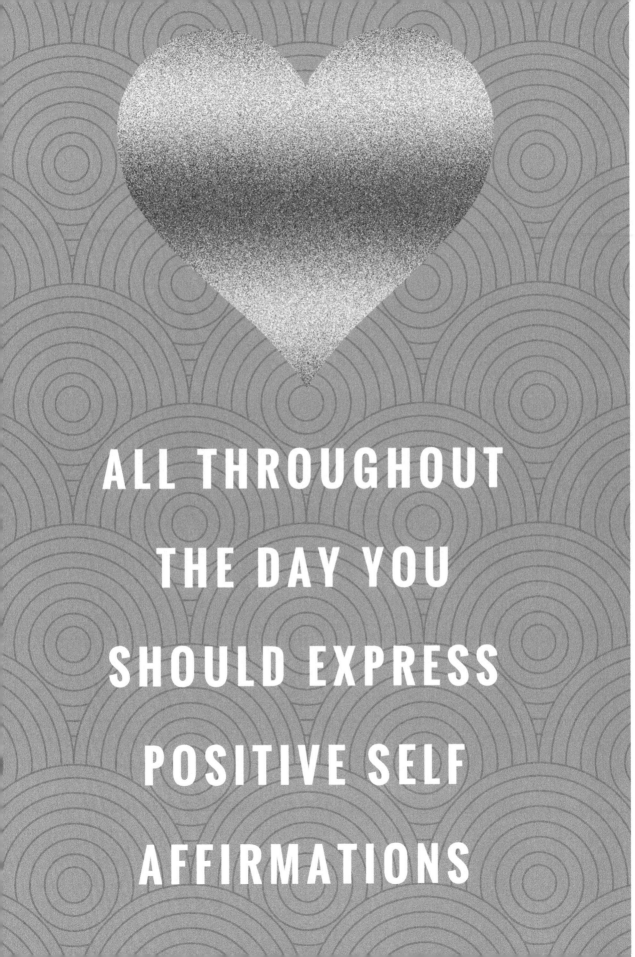

ALL THROUGHOUT THE DAY YOU SHOULD EXPRESS POSITIVE SELF AFFIRMATIONS

YOU ARE

BEAUTIFUL

INSIDE AND OUT

NEVER GIVE UP

YOU HAVE

EVERYTHING IT TAKES

TO BE GLAMOROUS

PUT SOME LIPSTICK ON AND BOSS UP

Pretty Pennies

SET FINANCIAL GOALS & KEEP TRACK OF EVERY PENNY

DEVELOP A BUDGET & STICK TO IT

MAKE A LIST OF ALL YOUR MONTHLY BILLS
& THEIR DUE DATES TO KEEP PAYMENTS ON TIME

FUND YOUR RETIREMENT

START AN EMERGENCY FUND
(INITIAL GOAL: 6 MNTHS INCOME)

PAY DOWN YOUR DEBT

EAT OUT LESS

NO IMPULSE PURCHASES

LEARN THE ART OF BARGAIN SHOPPING
THRIFTING & COUPONING

You Deserve Financial Freedom

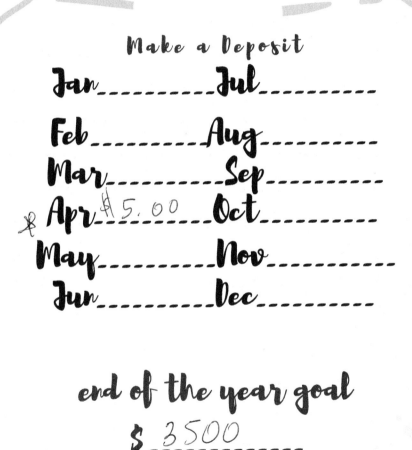

Make a Deposit

Jan _____ Jul _____

Feb _____ Aug _____

Mar _____ Sep _____

$ Apr $5.00 ___ Oct _____

May _____ Nov _____

Jun _____ Dec _____

end of the year goal
$ 3500 _____

Express Yourself...

I must not be so distracted by wanting things on my own time that I forget to be present, give back, pray, and truly trust God. Remember that it takes work to renew the mind. What I fill my heart, mind, and body with is what i'll become. I must improve my life and my attitude towards life.

1/9/18

4/29/19

Express Yourself...

Waking up at 5:30 a.m. to a clean house was the best feeling. I am proud of where things are going in life. I've constantly been praying for energy and I finally had that prayer answered today. God is not going to allow me to fail. I must continue to work and he will bless my efforts.

Express Yourself...

The season of Spring is coming to an end soon and I have been praying for God to really work through me. I want to see major break-throughs in my life over the next few weeks. A boldness that's lead by pure peace and acceptance of who I am and what God wants for my life. I need to truly dive into the spirits of fruit that God says there are no laws against. Belive in yourself Chrystal You are never alone you have been made new. Claim, accept, appreciate and trust that. Have faith and pray over all your steps in life. Your father will God you.

Express Yourself...

Being transparent about my feelings and thoughts isn't always easy lord. I struggle with trusting probably because I haven't always been trusting. I struggle with letting things go. I struggle with performance anxiety. But I want to thank you for loving me ~~despite~~ despite the fact that I struggle to see the greatness you have blessed me with. It's time to really release the negative self talk and focus truly on being the best version of myself. Accepting love forgiving, affirming blessings because they are deserved and earn at times. I love you for giving me another day of life

#GIRLBOSS

IN STYLE

VOGUE

CHANEL

Express Yourself...

Today was so refreshing. After repenting yesterday and following up on the meaning of soulties, I noticed that I maybe holding on to energy that wasn't meant for me. I was holding a grudge with myself for messing up my goals and promises to myself. More people have been distancing themselves taking time for themselves and I realized that I probably should do the same. I took a break from my business social media, got back into my bible plans and really started trying to enjoy the day, and my life. I applyed for a job and got an instant response. Crazy I dyed my hair and I love it and me and rye spent time together to day

Express Yourself...

was truly refreshing. I'm egan to continue pushing forward. God truly is blessing me and ~~the~~ my prayers ~~that~~ are being answered what an amazing feeling. energy restored, financial blessings coming, getting out not letting fear hold me, my life is important.

THE
DREAMPRINT

LET YOUR DREAMS BE THE BLUEPRINT OF YOUR LIFE

Faith | base

11.13 God lead me back
to faith building
in my
scriptures
Hebrews
11.13
to the
simple
Abundance
Faith was
the key
word
9/6

fruts of the Spirit

small steps

January
Self control

June
♡
Love

Family Household

Fall activities

Corn maze

watch geese flying south for the winter

* petting zoo

* Rice Krispie treats

* Farmer's Market

Mother

Role

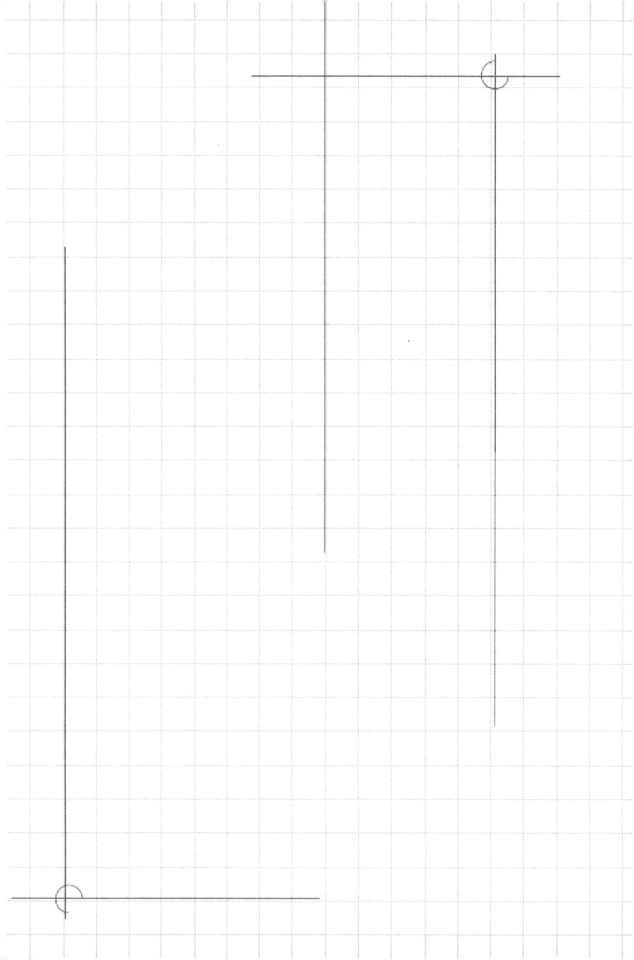

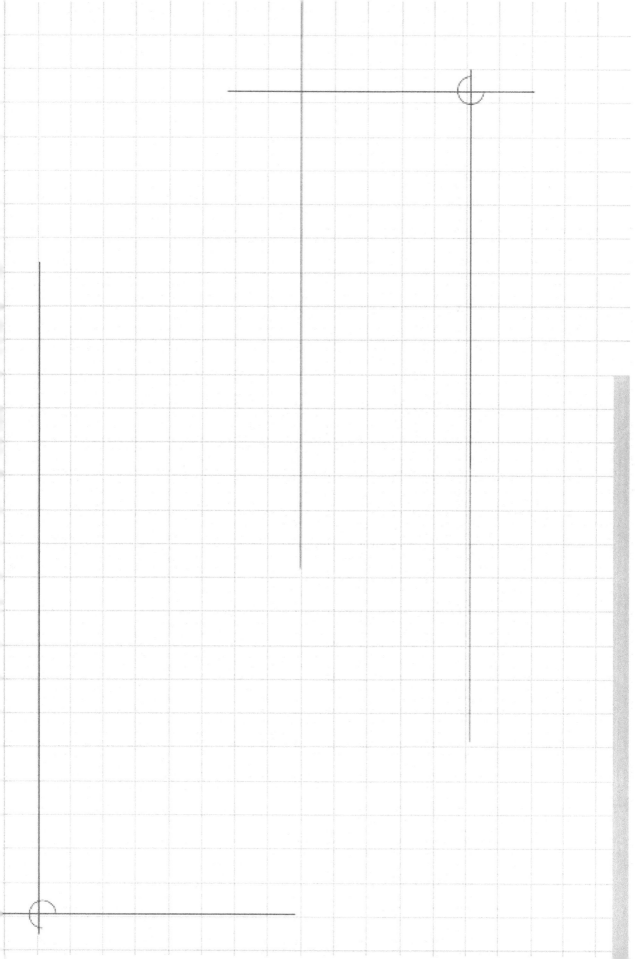

Daily Gratitude Journal

POSITIVE AFFIRMATION

When I ~~scar~~ sacrifice it's between me and God

THE BEST PART OF MY DAY

Begining to clean my room and being present in the shower.

I AM GRATEFUL FOR

I'm grateful for having enough to purchase things from the store. Enjoying icecream sundaes with my son. friends who trust me enough to ~~confind~~ confide in me.

MOOD/ENERGY

mood a bit cranky with people while out but my energy has improved. I felt so drag the past week but things are looking up!

Daily Gratitude Journal

POSITIVE AFFIRMATION

DATE: 4 /28 /19

Don't get give up and don't worry release and work hard.

THE BEST PART OF MY DAY

Walking to the store (getting out for fresh air).
Team work cleaning the kitchen with Aryes.

I AM GRATEFUL FOR

Long baths

MOOD/ENERGY

Highs and lows but I was able to get my quiz done, long bath, and a smoothie.
Ending the day proud of accomplishments

Daily Gratitude Journal

POSITIVE AFFIRMATION   DATE: 4 / 29 / 19

I am blessed

THE BEST PART OF MY DAY

Waking up to a clean home, having the energy to complete most of the things on my to do list.

I AM GRATEFUL FOR

Answered prayers
Zen wax cubes

MOOD/ENERGY

Vibrant I felt so alive today.
"Refreshed"

Daily Gratitude Journal

POSITIVE AFFIRMATION

DATE: 5 / 2 / 19

Be aware of your pride.

THE BEST PART OF MY DAY

Bible study I feel that God instantly answer
-ed my prayer and Guided me on how to
come closer to him.
" What's next"

John "1:12" God number

I AM GRATEFUL FOR

Peaceful days, and good weather.
Picking back up on bible study
so needed.
Time with God is a blessing

MOOD/ENERGY

Serene

Daily Gratitude Journal

POSITIVE AFFIRMATION

DATE: 5 / 3 /19

I have all I need for the day
it's a blessing to even be able to have
wants.

THE BEST PART OF MY DAY

Not lingering in negativity... Next time things
don't go my way I want to keep that to
myself not everything needs to be shared.
Be kind be loving be positive.

I AM GRATEFUL FOR

God ideas. When I hear gods voice I
must trust and have faith in the directions
he gives and follow them.

MOOD/ENERGY

Rocky Road
ups and downs but the day ended well.
Released negative energy, explored creativity.
appreciated nature and ate a wonderful
meal.

Daily Gratitude Journal

POSITIVE AFFIRMATION

DATE: 7 / 1 / 2019

I am qualified through God

THE BEST PART OF MY DAY

Getting my Nail tech license in the mail

I AM GRATEFUL FOR

Food to eat, a roof over our heads, my, car, Gods continual blessings, my new young nails kit!!

MOOD/ENERGY

optimistic   medium flow

Daily Gratitude Journal

POSITIVE AFFIRMATION

Move, explore, get back to nature, and enjoy life

THE BEST PART OF MY DAY

Today was so great I can't just name 1 good thing that happened. Me and Rye went to the park (explored the creek and trees). We went to get fresh juice from first watch and enjoyed jerk.

I AM GRATEFUL FOR

New energy. Taking time to evaluate mood changes helped me pin point the root of my mood shift.

MOOD/ENERGY

Positive mood high energy... opened to changes.

Daily Gratitude Journal

POSITIVE AFFIRMATION

DATE: 2 / 9 / 20

I fucks with myself

THE BEST PART OF MY DAY

I AM GRATEFUL FOR

coffee, challenges that push me out of my comfort zone

MOOD/ENERGY

Mood: shes gonna get it

When you plan your day ahead of time it shows a great deal of self appreciation. You are able to prioritize your activities, and delegate what is important enough to get your time. You accept that the power of Preparation is not in controlling your day's outcome, but all in understanding the productiveness of a sound mind.

For the next two weeks
take the time
to plan out each of your
days.
Enjoy keeping track of your
appointments, checking off
your To Do List, and
picking out
the perfect pair of heels to
complete
your outfit of the day!

Have a Great
Day Beautiful!

Date | / | | 2024

- [ ] love yourself
- [ ] think positive
- [ ] pay it forward
- [ ] positive self affirmation
- [ ] 1 hour social media break

Appointments

To Do List

: --

: --

: --

: --

: --

Notes

Tomorrow's OOTD:

Have a Great Day Beautiful!

Date | / 2 | 2024

- [ ] love yourself
- [ ] think positive
- [ ] pay it forward
- [ ] positive self affirmation
- [ ] 1 hour social media break

Appointments

- : ------------------------------
- : ------------------------------
- : ------------------------------
- : ------------------------------
- : ------------------------------

To Do List

- Schedule Board
- Go to school (loan forms)
- Call the doc. (MH)
- Mondays or Tuesdays or Sundays

Notes

Tomorrow's OOTD:

Have a Great Day Beautiful!

Date / 1 3 / 2024

- [ ] love yourself
- [ ] think positive
- [ ] pay it forward
- [ ] positive self affirmation
- [ ] 1 hour social media break

Appointments

To Do List

- ....
- ....
- ....
- ....
- ....

Notes

Tomorrow's OOTD:

Have a Great Day Beautiful!

Date / / 4   / 2024

- [ ] love yourself
- [ ] think positive
- [ ] pay it forward
- [ ] positive self affirmation
- [ ] 1 hour social media break

Appointments

: ----------------------------------
: ----------------------------------
: ----------------------------------
: ----------------------------------
: ----------------------------------

To Do List

Notes

Tomorrow's OOTD:

Have a Great
Day Beautiful!

☐ love yourself
☐ think positive
☐ pay it forward
☐ positive self affirmation
☐ 1 hour social media break

Date 1 / 5 / 2024

Appointments

To Do List

: -------------------------------
: -------------------------------
: -------------------------------
: -------------------------------
: -------------------------------

Notes

Tomorrow's OOTD:

Have a Great
Day Beautiful!

Date ' / 6   / 2024

☐ love yourself
☐ think positive
☐ pay it forward
☐ positive self affirmation
☐ 1 hour social media break

Appointments

To Do List

: --
: --
: --
: --
: --

Notes

Tomorrow's OOTD:

Have a Great Day Beautiful!

Date | / 7   12°²⁴

☐ love yourself
☐ think positive
☐ pay it forward
☐ positive self affirmation
☐ 1 hour social media break

Appointments

: ----------------------------------
: ----------------------------------
: ----------------------------------
: ----------------------------------
: ----------------------------------

To Do List

Notes

Tomorrow's OOTD:

Have a Great Day Beautiful!

Date / / 8 / 2024

- [ ] love yourself
- [ ] think positive
- [ ] pay it forward
- [ ] positive self affirmation
- [ ] 1 hour social media break

Appointments

: -----------------------------------
: -----------------------------------
: -----------------------------------
: -----------------------------------
: -----------------------------------

To Do List

Notes

Tomorrow's OOTD:

Have a Great Day Beautiful!

Date | 9 | 2024

- [ ] love yourself
- [ ] think positive
- [ ] pay it forward
- [ ] positive self affirmation
- [ ] 1 hour social media break

Appointments

To Do List

: ----------------------------------
: ----------------------------------
: ----------------------------------
: ----------------------------------
: ----------------------------------

Notes

Tomorrow's OOTD:

Have a Great
Day Beautiful!

Date / 1 10   12024

☐ love yourself
☐ think positive
☐ pay it forward
☐ positive self affirmation
☐ 1 hour social media break

Appointments

To Do List

: ------------------------------------
: ------------------------------------
: ------------------------------------
: ------------------------------------
: ------------------------------------

Notes

Tomorrow's OOTD:

Have a Great
Day Beautiful!

Date / / II   / 2024

- [ ] love yourself
- [ ] think positive
- [ ] pay it forward
- [ ] positive self affirmation
- [ ] 1 hour social media break

Appointments

To Do List

: -----------------------------------
: -----------------------------------
: -----------------------------------
: -----------------------------------
: -----------------------------------

Notes

Tomorrow's OOTD:

Have a Great Day Beautiful!

Date / 1 / 2   / 2024

- [ ] love yourself
- [ ] think positive
- [ ] pay it forward
- [ ] positive self affirmation
- [ ] 1 hour social media break

Appointments

: --
: --
: --
: --
: --

To Do List

Notes

Tomorrow's OOTD:

Have a Great Day Beautiful!

Date 1 / 13 / 2024

☐ love yourself
☐ think positive
☐ pay it forward
☐ positive self affirmation
☐ 1 hour social media break

Appointments

: ------------------------------------
: ------------------------------------
: ------------------------------------
: ------------------------------------
: ------------------------------------

To Do List

Notes

Tomorrow's OOTD:

Have a Great Day Beautiful!

Date 1 / 14   12024

Appointments

: -----------------------------------
: -----------------------------------
: -----------------------------------
: -----------------------------------
: -----------------------------------

To Do List

Notes

Tomorrow's OOTD:

Charms

First set
Charms Concepts
The brain - mind set   amygdala

Cranes, brain, brain cells, serotonin, will power

First collection brings awareness of how important
thoughts are.

Set: photo shoot   Brain stimulants
                       Positive herbs

paper cranes
    long braids   clients will respond
    charms   to my post
    and beads   when I repost I
                       will fill up the
                       images with
                       unique styles

    origami set all charms unique styles

    cranes, boat paper air plane swane

    wine charms — wine oil

MANIFEST

DREAM BIG

ON YOUR DREAM BOARD

Personal selfcare / Entertainment

Once a month movies

Spa (Family Membership)

Gym Membership

Dine Out at a resturant 1x per
month or 1 cooking class

200$

Homeschool for Rye

Classes

DREAM BIG

ON YOUR DREAM BOARD

Curly to straight

✻ pre shampoo only to the scalp

✻ hair steamer

2 braid clients

Chris D[...] (signature)

9/7/19

Reality check

I made more working for myself than working at any other job, in one day.
$125 vs. 70$ Average at most
recent job

I didn't have to leave my home.
~~Great~~ Grateful goodwill taught me
so much that it's time for me
to step out and do what I'm passi
-onate about.

you are

capable of

doing amazing

things

BE CLOTHED IN CONFIDENCE

-

IT IS THE MOST ALLURING THING IN YOUR CLOSET

Did

You

Love

Yourself

Today?

Each and every
day you are required to
love and respect
yourself.
Do not leave
any room for
self doubt and pity.
Instead of focusing on
what you can't do, focus
only on what you can do.
Who you are, and what
you have to offer this world is
important.

Date: 4/27

How did you love yourself today?

I began cleaning my room because I know clutter does not bring peace to my mind.

I took a shower and thought of how amazing our Creator is. He created water both for cleansing and drinking. I'm grateful to have clean water to bathe and drink.

Date:

How did you love yourself today?

Hydrated my body with coconut water.

Dived into my creativity pool and designed some nails. Listened to God and found

peace with my day.

Date: 1/12/2020

How did you love yourself today?

I gave myself a pedicure. My toes were jacked lol. But I figured doing them wasn't really a big deal. I realized taking time for myself to do little things like painting my toes show that I care about myself.

Date: 5/8/20

How did you love yourself today?

Today I drank water 2 jugs, exercised, listened to the bible, meal prepped, walked, washed Ayes and my hair, waist trained, Acknowledge Negative traits, and Plan summer goals. Self care and self evaluation! I will work on being boastful, bitter, and oversharing!

How did you love yourself today?

Leaving out was the way I loved and showed up for myself today. Showering, getting dressed and leaving my home gave me a sense of freedom. Facing my fears and being comfortable with be alone while out was a nice boost in my confidence.

Date:

How did you love yourself today?

_____

_____

_____

_____

_____

Date:

How did you love yourself today?

_____

_____

_____

_____

_____

Date:

How did you love yourself today?

_____

_____

_____

_____

_____

BAD

HABITS DIE HARD...

But don't let that stop you from planning the perfect funeral for them. More often than not, your bad habits are brought to your attention by a loved one or friend before you recognize them on your own. This does not mean you are unaware of your own behaviors; sometimes others have the ability to see you more plainly than you see yourself. You may even believe that the observer is being a bit harsh, don't take it that way, its not always easy to hear what you're doing wrong. However, you shouldn't let "easily offended" be associated with your existence either. Instead, use that advice and rid yourself of anything that darkens your glamorous spirit.

ASHES TO ASHES
LAY YOUR BAD HABITS TO REST

Waiting for
Others to
provide me w/
What I need

Negative
Self
Talk

DUST TO DUST
LAY YOUR BAD HABITS TO REST

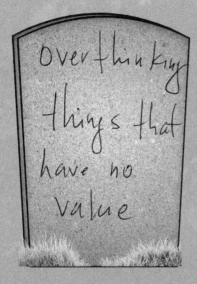

overthinking things that have no value

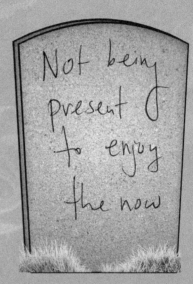

Not being present to enjoy the now

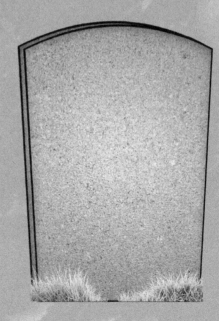

What can you do to strengthen 3 of your most important relationships, and what are your expectations after doing so?

What is your passion?

Are you where you want to be in life, if not what steps do you plan to take in order to get there?

What is a current hindrance in your life, and how do you plan on overcoming that obstacle?

DAILY Dream BOARD

MUST HAVES FOR THE DAY

RELATIONSHIPS

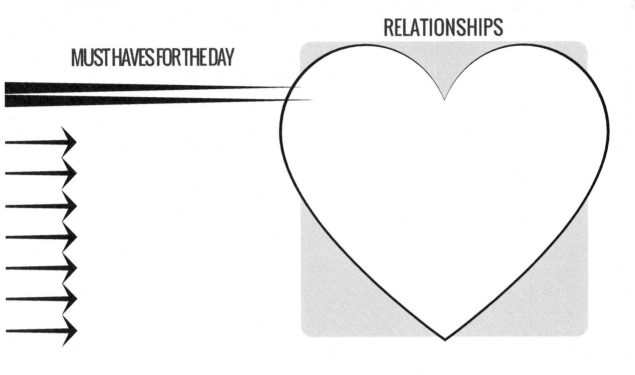

TODAY I WILL MANIFEST

DAILY Dream BOARD

RELATIONSHIPS

MUST HAVES FOR THE DAY

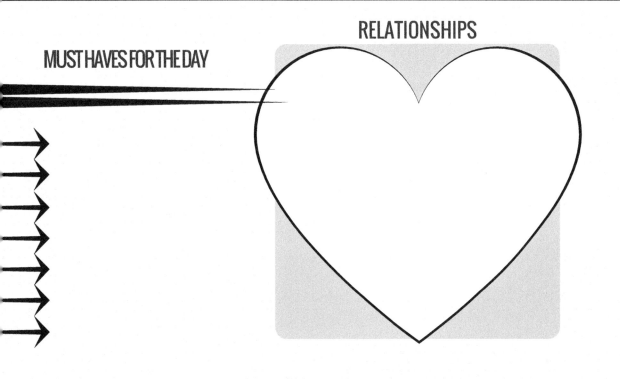

TODAY I WILL MANIFEST

DAILY Dream BOARD

RELATIONSHIPS

MUST HAVES FOR THE DAY

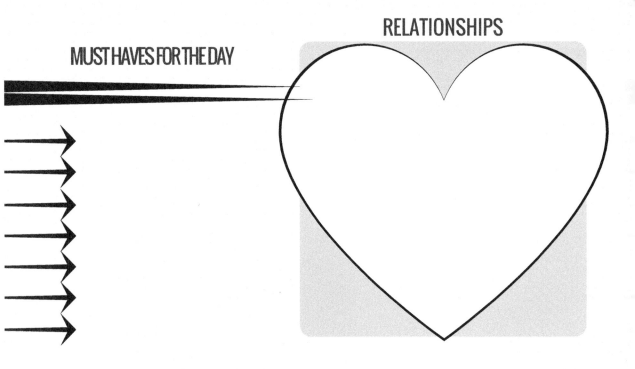

TODAY I WILL MANIFEST

DAILYDreamBOARD

MUST HAVES FOR THE DAY

RELATIONSHIPS

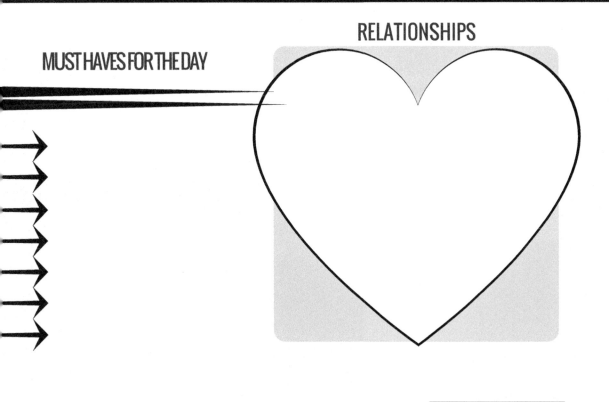

TODAY I WILL MANIFEST

DAILY Dream BOARD

RELATIONSHIPS

MUST HAVES FOR THE DAY

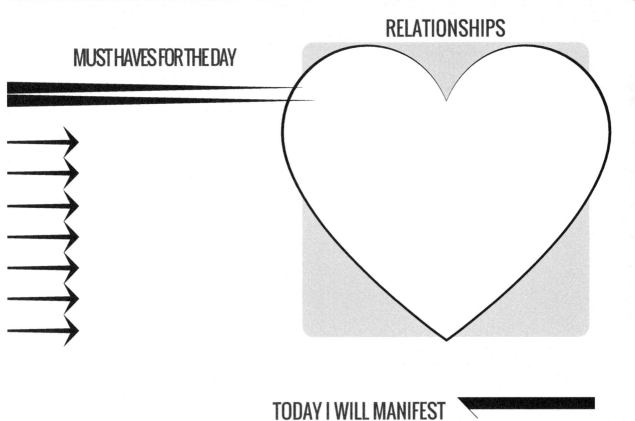

TODAY I WILL MANIFEST

DAILY Dream BOARD

MUST HAVES FOR THE DAY

RELATIONSHIPS

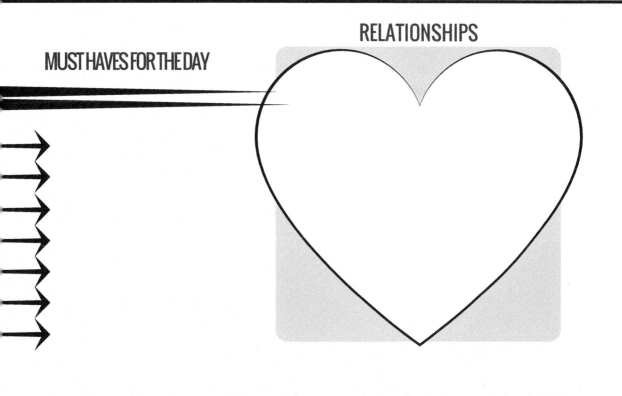

TODAY I WILL MANIFEST

DAILY Dream BOARD

RELATIONSHIPS

MUST HAVES FOR THE DAY

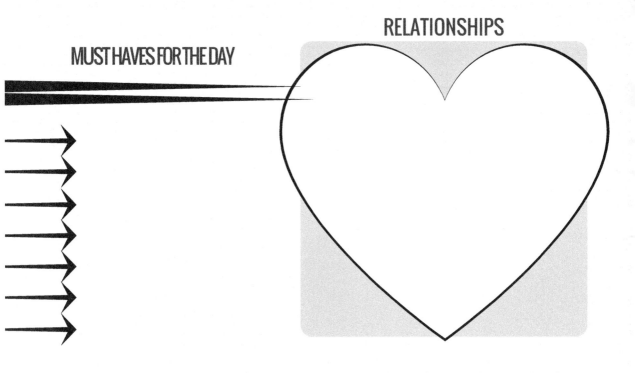

TODAY I WILL MANIFEST

DAILY Dream BOARD

MUST HAVES FOR THE DAY

RELATIONSHIPS

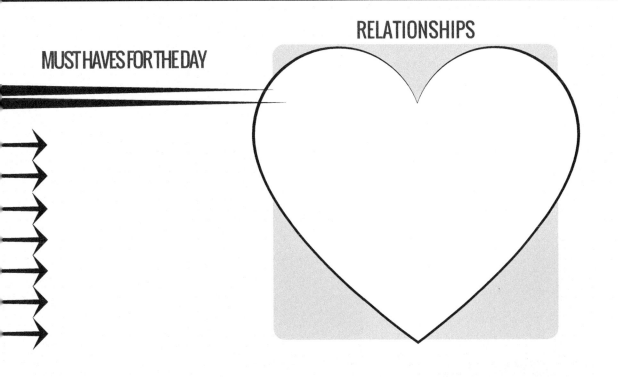

TODAY I WILL MANIFEST

Build your Dream Life

DREAM CAREER
(INSERT PICTURE HERE)

DREAM HOUSE
(INSERT PICTURE HERE)

Build your Dream Life

QUALIFICATIONS NEEDED

QUALIFICATIONS NEEDED

Build your Dream Life

DREAM CAR
(INSERT PICTURE HERE)

SOUL MATE
(INSERT PICTURE HERE)

Build your Dream Life

QUALIFICATIONS NEEDED

SELF PREPARATION

Event & Travel Planning

Vacation

DESTINATION:_____

DESIRED DATE:_____

LODGING & FEES:_____

AIRFARE/TRAVEL FEES:_____

VACATION GUEST:_____

VACATION BUDGET:_____

Date Night
PARTY OF ONE

DATE TO TREAT YOURSELF:_____

MOVIE___ DINNER___ NIGHT ON THE TOWN___

DATE NIGHT OUTFIT:_____
_____

LIPSTICK OF THE NIGHT:_____

DON'T FORGET TO TAKE THE PERFECT SELFIE!

Ladies Night

ROLL CALL: _____
_____

VENUE: _____
_____

SIGNATURE DRINK: _____

PUMPS & PURSE: _____
_____

DESIRED DATE: _____

5 Ways to be More Confident

1. Stop comparing yourself to others and focus on how great you are.

2. Don't be an over thinker, go with the flow, and leave the anxieties at the door. There is no need to worry about things you can't control.

3. Love yourself, there is only one you, and you make the world go round.

4. Do what makes you happy!

5. Keep a positive mindset, don't focus on negativity, and acknowledge the best in every situation.

CONFIDENCE

=paid for your pa$$ion=

Here's how to get started ✔ ✔

Write a business plan
You can visit
your local
government
websites for
small business
resources

Choose
a name
& become legal by
obtaining the
proper licenses &
permits

Open a business
bank account

Invest in branding
your business

Set up your desired
methods for
receiving payment

Just in case you need a little inspiration

Virtual Assistant
Customer Service
Jewelry Maker
Personal Trainer
Blogger
Mentor
Tutor
Meal Prep & Delivery
eBay Seller
Pet Groomer - Dog Walker
Tailor
Pet Sitter - House Sitter
Maid Service
Resume Writer
Personal Shopper
Personal Stylist
Web Designer
Candle Maker
Event/Wedding Planner
Interior Decorator
Web Content Writer
Branding Consultant
Homemade Crafts
Sell Self Help ebooks
Sell Downloadable Content
Social Media Manager

WEALTH

=$UCCE$$ORIE$=

SOCIAL MEDIA = DAILY POSTING

CUSTOMER INTERACTION

DEVELOP A -BRAND STRATEGY- FOR A SLEEK AND COHESIVE LOOK THAT WILL BE APPEALING TO THE EYE OF THE CONSUMER
-
LOGO
WEBSITE - DOMAIN NAME
BUSINESS CARDS

BUDGET PLAN

TABLET/COMPUTER

BUSINESS PHONE LINE (THERE IS AN APP FOR THAT)

BUSINESS EMAIL

ACCOUNTING SOFTWARE

Things you Need to Accessorize your success

A PLANNER TO STAY ORGANIZED

WEALTH

MANIFEST YOUR MONEY HONEY YOU HAVE THE POWER!

MANIFEST

1001
1-23/5678

DATE

PAY
TO THE ORDER OF

$

DOLLARS

Security
Features
Details on
Back

MP

FOR

⑈1234567891: 000⑈222⑈2211" 1001

GLAM GUIDE
WRITING
Prompts

My most joyous life moment...

The money is coming 7/2/20
Don't stress the funds will come

My best life lesson and why?

Recently, I've discovered that fear can limit your preception of opportunities. "It's always worse in your mind than in reality. Speaking negatively doesn't leave room for confidence to venture to the next steps, solve issues, or live fearlessly. we're never starting over ~~there~~ we're moving forward with experience.

My current energy drainer...

On my next day off I want to...

If I had One Million Dollars...

My strengths & weaknesses?

1 weakness lack of self control
    (mostly my mouth especially w/ men)

My Legacy...

Try These
Money Managing
Tools to
Keep your
Glam Buck$
in check

MONTHLY
Glam Buck$ Management

Month: _____ **year:** _____

Starting Balance:_____Starting Debt:_____
Monthly Income:_____

Mortgage/Rent:_/_____	Credit Card 1: April 20 2019
Taxes:_____	Credit Card 2: 8216
Owners/Renters Ins:_____	Credit Card 3:_____
Home Repairs:_____	Extra:_____
Electric:_/___75_____	Extra:_____
Gas:_____	Unexpected:_____
Sewer/Trash:_____	
Internet/Cable:_____	**Monthly Savings Plan**
Phone:____60_____	
Grocery:_____	Starting Balance:_____
Charity:_____	Monthly Goal:_____
Car Payment:_____	Ending Balance:_____
Car Insurance:_225.33_____	
Gas/Transportation:_____	**Next Months Savings Goal**
Maintenance:_____	
Entertainment:_____	Amount:_____
Clothing:_____	
Child(ren):_____	Goal Met: Yes( ) No( )
Medical Insurance:_____	*you deserve a*
Medical Office Visits:_____	*Financially Stable*
Feminine Necessities:_____	*Future!*

MONTHLY
Glam Buck$ Management

Month: _____ year: _____

Starting Balance:_____Starting Debt:_____
Monthly Income:_____

Mortgage/Rent:__102_____	Credit Card 1:_____
Taxes:_____	Credit Card 2:_____
Owners/Renters Ins:_____	Credit Card 3:_____
Home Repairs:_____	Extra:_____
Electric:_____	Extra:_____
Gas:_____	Unexpected:_____
Sewer/Trash:_____	
Internet/Cable:_____	*Monthly Savings Plan*
Phone:_____	Starting Balance:_____
Grocery:_____	Monthly Goal:_____
Charity:_____	Ending Balance:_____
Car Payment:_____	
Car Insurance:_____	*Next Months Savings Goal*
Gas/Transportation:_____	Amount:_____
Maintenance:_____	
Entertainment:_____	Goal Met: Yes( ) No( )
Clothing:_____	
Child(ren):_____	*you deserve a*
Medical Insurance:_____	*financially stable*
Medical Office Visits:_____	*future!*
Feminine Necessities:_____	

MONTHLY
Glam Buck$ Management

Month: Year:

Starting Balance:_____ Starting Debt:_____
Monthly Income:_____

Mortgage/Rent:_____	Credit Card 1: 133.31 _____ Amm
Taxes:_____	Credit Card 2:_____
Owners/Renters Ins:_____	Credit Card 3:_____
Home Repairs:_____	Extra:_____
Electric:_____	Extra:_____
Gas:_____	Unexpected:_____
Sewer/Trash:_____	
Internet/Cable:_____	Monthly Savings Plan
Phone:_____	
Grocery:_____	Starting Balance:_____
Charity:_____	Monthly Goal:_____
Car Payment:_____	Ending Balance:_____
Car Insurance:_____	
Gas/Transportation:_____	Next Months Savings Goal
Maintenance:_____	Amount:_____
Entertainment:_____	Goal Met: Yes( ) No( )
Clothing:_____	
Child(ren):_____	you deserve a
Medical Insurance:_____	Financially stable
Medical Office Visits:_____	Future!
Feminine Necessities:_____	

Hey Beautiful,
Separate your Glam
Buck$ each month by using
a ca$h envelope system.
                    -popo

ca$h Envelope System

A cash envelope system is an easy way to divide your Glam Buck$ and keep an organized budget. All spending with this system is done in cash. Each category has it's own envelope to help keep your spending separate from your Fixed Monthly Expenses, which should remain in your account for auto-pay. Be sure to properly manage all withdrawals to avoid overdrafting your account.

Cash Envelopes can be used for: Groceries, Gas, Cosmetics, Recreation etc. Once you have depleted your budget for a particular envelope you must practice discipline by not dipping into your savings.
Fixed Monthly Expenses: Rent/Mortgage, Utilities, Car Payment, Cell Phone.

THINK
GREEN
GIRL

DO NOT SUCCUMB TO THE THOUGHT OF DEBT IT HAS THE ABILITY TO IMPOVERISH YOUR MINDSET

DEBT PAYMENT PLAN

DEBT: Andrews Federal credit loan

TOTAL AMOUNT:

MINIMUM PAYMENT:

INTEREST RATE:

DATE	STARTING BALANCE	PAYMENT	REMAINING BALANCE

DEBT PAYMENT PLAN

DEBT: cApital One credit cards

TOTAL AMOUNT: 1472.00

MINIMUM PAYMENT: 272.00
50.00 per m/

INTEREST RATE:

DATE	STARTING BALANCE	PAYMENT	REMAINING BALANCE
7/20			

DEBT PAYMENT PLAN

DEBT:

TOTAL AMOUNT:

MINIMUM PAYMENT:

INTEREST RATE: N/A

DATE	STARTING BALANCE	PAYMENT	REMAINING BALANCE

DEBT PAYMENT PLAN

DEBT:

TOTAL AMOUNT:

MINIMUM PAYMENT:

INTEREST RATE:

DATE	STARTING BALANCE	PAYMENT	REMAINING BALANCE

MANIFESTATION *Maven*

10/23/19 ✱ 2/18/20

DATE

YOUR DESIRE

Increase Income

PLACE OF PEACE Prayer Room

TIME SPENT

CURRENT MOOD

DOUBT FREE

WHAT IS ON YOUR MIND?

How to be my brand, to create finanical freedom.

(God)

TELL THE ~~UNIVERSE~~ IT IS YOURS

Sorry I glitched ((herbal) ~~holistic~~ brand

☑ Food handlers

☐ tax Id #

☐ retail license/liquor lic se

☐ Tincture filled chocolates

MANIFESTATION *Maven*

DATE

YOUR DESIRE

WHAT IS ON YOUR MIND?

PLACE OF PEACE

TIME SPENT

CURRENT MOOD

DOUBT FREE

TELL THE UNIVERSE IT IS YOURS

MANIFESTATION *Maven*

YOUR DESIRE

Never stop Exploring

PLACE OF PEACE Prayer room

TIME SPENT

CURRENT MOOD intrigued

DOUBT FREE

WHAT IS ON YOUR MIND?

wondering how to break out of my shell.

TELL THE UNIVERSE IT IS YOURS

Money flowing in
Less fear of exploring

Don't Be That Girl

WOMEN EMPOWER WOMEN

EMPOWERED WOMEN HAVE A BETTER CHANCE AT SUCCESS WHEN THEY ARE SURROUNDED BY SUPPORT

NEVER HARBOR HATRED

DO NOT BE FILLED WITH ENVY

DO NOT LET JEALOUSY LEAD YOU ON A PATH TO DESTRUCTION

SHARE THE SPOTLIGHT

WOMEN LOVE COMPLIMENTS - BE GENEROUS

REMEMBER EVERYTHING IS NOT A COMPETITION

KEEP DREAMING
KEEP BELIEVING
KEEP MANIFESTING
YOU ARE THE
AUTHOR AND
CREATOR OF YOUR
GLAMOROUS LIFE

Love Always,

Yvette E. Tariq

MEET THE AUTHOR
Yvette E. Tariq

YVETTE E. TARIQ IS A NATIVE WASHINGTONIAN, WIFE TO BESTSELLING AUTHOR MU TARIQ, MOTHER TO ACTIVE 9 YEAR OLD EVRENCE, CERTIFIED LIFE COACH, AND CO-FOUNDER OF THE TARIQSPHERE. SHE IS THE BEST SELLING AUTHOR OF "#LABS VOL. 1 THE CHRONICLES OF MISS MONIQUE" A STORY BASED ON REAL LIFE EVENTS; AND IS AT IT AGAIN WITH "DREAM BOARD IN A BOOK." YVETTE INVITES YOU TO SHARE IN THE JOYS OF HER SOUL WITH THIS PROJECT, HAVING DESIGNED EACH AND EVERY PAGE TO AIDE YOU IN THE MANIFESTATION OF YOUR GLAMOROUS LIFE.

CPSIA information can be obtained
at www.ICGtesting.com
Printed in the USA
BVOW05s0228190917
495265BV00024B/66/P